Minutes of Love
In The Hours of Life

Selected Poems: 1993-2004

Oscar R. Rocha

iUniverse, Inc.

New York   Bloomington

Minutes Of Love In The Hours Of Life
Selected Poems: 1993-2004

iUniverse books may be ordered through booksellers or by contacting:

iUniverse
1663 Liberty Drive
Bloomington, IN 47403
www.iuniverse.com
1-800-Authors (1-800-288-4677)

ISBN: 978-1-4401-5188-0 (pbk)
ISBN: 978-1-4401-5189-7 (cloth)
ISBN: 978-1-4401-5190-3 (ebook)

Library of Congress Control Number: 2009931975

Printed in the United States of America

iUniverse rev. date: 7/16/09

Contents

(WHENEVER THE POEM IS UNTITLED, THE FIRST
SENTENCE OF THE POEM HAS BEEN WRITTEN AS
REFERENCE)

QUEST, CONQUER IT, IT'S THE END OF YOUR PAIN.........1

IT'S JUST ANOTHER ONE 3

BLIND ALLEY (OF HOLY WARS)...................................5

WIND BLOWING AGAINST YOU...................................7

CELESTIAL STRANGER..9

HEARTACHE 11

HANGING...13

FALLS OVER FLOWED 15

BLIND EYES NEED NO TRUST..17

AS MY "THIRD BREAST" PAINFULLY EVOLVES, ...19

REACH FOR NIETZSCHE? 21

LUGEN UND DAS ICH * (CATASTROPHE AT BOSNIA)....23

NEOPHOBIA (1)..25

ZADOK 27

DAS ICH *..29

NEOPHOBIA (2) 31

PRUDENCE...33

A SECRET FOR THE BEAUTY 35

A NEW ROSE IN MY HEAD?...37

PERTAINING TO OUR YOUTH 39

LUSCIOUS JORDAN ALMOND 41

THE ELEVENTH ANGEL (BY YOUR SIDE) 43

THE ELEVENTH ANGEL (IN DARKNESS) 45

MANKIND IS CALLED 47

LET HER VIBES PENETRATE YOU 49

LET HER VIBES PENETRATE 51

NATURE'S SECRET 53

THIRST: CAGED TONGUES 55

IN DARKEST CONSCIENCE 57

TREEMAN, A 59

AS I RAN THROUGH THE RAIN, THE SAME RAIN
THAT SHOWERS MOUNT OLYMPUS 61

WHO IS WHO 63

NATURA 65

BY THE RIVER 67

LEAVING SEVILLA 69

ARRIVING 71

LEAVING BADAJOZ 73

THE PRAISED MISCONCEPTION 75

ON THIS EARTH, THE GROUND EXTENDS.......................77

THE PENDULUM AND THE BANSHEE UNDER THE
FULL MOON 79

AT THE BAR (IN SOME CONCERT @ THE 930 CLUB)......81

GIFT OF LOVE 83

THE SHADOW OF DEATH LEAVES 85

TIME STILL THROUGH SPACE 87

PAST THE GREY ORACLE'S DWELLING CAVE 89

FLESHY CLOTH, HEART THROBBLES 91

DEW FALLS, A CARESS 93

GEORGETOWN BRIDGE 95

FIRST BREADTH 97

TIME SLOWS DOWN, ...99

OH ! FUTURE WHAT COULD THEE HOLD FOR ME (1)..101

OH ! FUTURE WHAT COULD THEE HOLD FOR ME (2)..103

TASTE 105

UNWANTED SECRETS.......................................107

COME NEAR 109

MUSE 2000 (FAR) 111

MUSE 2000 (CLOSE).....................................113

INVOCATING THE MUSE 115

MEMORIES FROM THE COMBAT ZONE (1) – AFGHANISTAN 2002 117

LET THE WIND TAKE YOU WHERE YOU WANT TO BE 119

MEMORIES FROM THE COMBAT ZONE (2) – AFGHANISTAN 2002 121

WOMACK ARMY MEDICAL CENTER..........................123

To my mother Marcela, and my
sister Ursula, for they are the
lights in my life

And to the muses who have
inspired those before me in my
family, from my father's side: Jose
Santos Chocano, and from my
mother's side: Modesto Molina.
May the muses continue to
inspire me and those to come

UNTITLED

Quest, conquer it, it's the end of your pain
Don't ask, you don't need help, you'll learn
Just do not be afraid,
You can be brave,
Step on the edge, you will see then that there is no edge
Pull out the sword from the stone
Put your armor on and terminate them

Nov. 19th 1993

UNTITLED

It's just another one
Think just not like anyone else
But anyone else it's just like it

Dec. 1993, Virginia

BLIND ALLEY (of Holy Wars)

Inside it
Can't get away from it
Troops of soldiers
Found the holy path
To administered justice
NO submission
Hallow guardian
Of court

Apr. 16th 1994, Virginia

UNTITLED

Wind blowing against you
Time running after you
Just can't forget your own memoirs
A path of sorrows
Cannot be found
Now, sleep
All you can sleep
Don't wake up or
Your dreams will connect in
To replace life existence
Unmasked your fears
Follow your soul and heart

Apr. 1994, Virginia

UNTITLED

Celestial stranger
Emerged in my unconscious cycle of life
Filled with joyous dedication to flourish
Fascinating creature

Jul. 2nd 1994, Virginia

HEARTACHE

Drag me into that abyss of yours,
To contempt my phobia of abashment,
Elucidate my inferior position,
So I would have to take this world,
See what they don't see
Feel what they don't feel
Fix what they can't fix
Sometimes it would be just easier
To be a Passionless Barbarian

Aug. 19th 1994, Virginia

UNTITLED

Hanging
Swinging
Is it over?
What is over?
This
What is this?
That's it
No, it's not
Who knows?
Just you

1994, Virginia

UNTITLED

Falls over flowed
People nailed it
Thought fixed it
Just ruined it,
Nothing can be done
Just live with it
Not too long
Because it's going to,
It's dying

Sep. 1994, Virginia

BLIND EYES NEED NO TRUST

And this is the chronicle of my life,
A beautiful creation with wonderful creatures
Celebrating their colors

I just get deeper into the black spots of
Everyday struggle for survival
So deep a penetration into my own darkness,
Sorrow, and feeling

Mercy is given to others
But I can't take that privilege,
For me it is an uncompleted fight
Against my own fears

Why? Because
Aliens are they that see no other than
A simple unclean rock cover with a
Delightful blindness

Sep. 04th 1994, Virginia

UNTITLED

As my "third breast" painfully evolves,
This voracious appetite of mine to pine for
The unknown,
The unlock door for the stand-still phase
Comes and stands,
Not painfully virtue, but that
Of this condemned soul,
With a majestic luxury for not
Speaking distasteful language

Oct. 11th 1994, Virginia

REACH FOR NIETZSCHE?

I hear steps, under and on top of me,
Tireless body, anxious mind,
Eyes trying to close,
But the hand always awake
This super powerful gift
As I close myself more,
The more I want to express,
The more I want to open

Oct. 16th 1994, Virginia

LUGEN UND DAS ICH * (Catastrophe at Bosnia)

As wounded bodies fall before each other,
Leaders of men break the silence
-PEACE- collaborators arrive and the number of corpses increases,

Serb children get loaded in the candy store
Serb adults get loaded in the supermarket,
Act like machines!
Act like puppets!
Act blind!
LIBERTE!

Dec. 02nd 1994, Virginia

* Inspired from the name of a song by the German band Das Ich. The name refers
to the Freudian term of the human ego, and lugen means lies. This song's name
made sense as both elements (ego and lies) are present whenever there are wars and
human suffering.

NEOPHOBIA (1)

Fortunate the man, whom in your passage met you,
Your patient composure gives you elegance,
The pathos of your creation
Endows faculties to your invincible creature

Generated from powers further than
The north and the cold

Outlandish creature, remote titan
Barbaric ruler of your musical atmosphere

Jan. 17th 1995, Virginia

ZADOK

Outburst of indescribable sensations,
About a soul in sorrow,
Suffocating pain has struggled,
It has reached out,
I have become sensible, it has
Completely neutralized my coldness and
Hatred towards outsiders

So afraid, even of my own
Body, that body and soul
The difference is felt

In this sensation, as I call it,
I find myself, as floating within
My body ready to leave to a
Dimension where I'll be less
Vulnerable, this of course cannot
Support the right of my
Anxious soul but the one of
A human mind

Feb. 02nd 1995, Virginia

DAS ICH *

My secret fears unraveled by the night,
As illusions my feelings stand-still,
I do not see with my eyes,
I feel the blood of my body
Boiling from the thousands eyes
Surrounding me, the shadows of the past,
My visions show a true love,
Skin in skin,
No words,
But an exchange of never ending
Movements that kill me,
But I will always be here hoping
That they will kill me again

Mar. 01st 1995, Virginia

* Inspired from the name of the German band Das Ich. The name refers to the Freudian term of the human ego.

NEOPHOBIA (2)

A majestic creature,
Ruler of her own musical atmosphere,
Her splendor goes further than the
North and the Cold

The Pathos of your creation had
Transformed me,
They had turned me
Into stone-still phase

Where once inside,
They had awakened me,
Only to admire your majestic splendor;
A penetration into my own
Darkness, sorrow and feeling
Delighted by you

Mar. 02nd 1995, Virginia

PRUDENCE

I've had consented
The contentment
Of this condemned soul,
An indomitable kind,
Pleasantly carelessness
As I approach
Your splendid atmosphere;
Unfold your blue eyes
And strike my midst
And pine for a passionless barbarian

Mar. 11th 1995, Virginia

A SECRET FOR THE BEAUTY

Oh! Fairest creature:
Comfort a friend,
With that genteel smile,
Your sublime intellectual brilliance
Enlightens my obscured soul

Motions from your limbs
Paralyzes my thoughts
Unspeakable your name
Remains in my lips,
For, it holds a special power

Mar. 13th 1995, Virginia

A NEW ROSE IN MY HEAD?

A whole phase takes place
Ready to emerge as it takes its shape
Only a smell has stayed
So powerful that the essence is
As the first time,
The mind, the senses
They had worked together
They had taken control of the state of mind
Arise this penetration,
Never-ending wonders, ready to
Conquer abashment and self-humiliation

Mar. 21st 1995, Virginia

PERTAINING TO OUR YOUTH

As I attain that prolific scent,
Build the pathos towards erudition,
A primus luminosity is felt for the
Very first time
Dark and grotesque shapes collapse
Therefore they create an eruption,
This generation must rise

Apr. 28th 1995, Virginia

LUSCIOUS JORDAN ALMOND

Lusty – Marvelous - Bodacious
Fragile, pure essence of infinity
Wonderful innocence

May 09th 1995, Virginia

THE ELEVENTH ANGEL (By Your Side)

A torch rips the inside of my senses and feelings,
Fragile soul, cease tormenting me,
Comfort this real-abstract mind,
With just a loving
Look,

I would be relieved receiving,
Your pure essence,
Infinity and wonderful innocence,
Acquired from you
Had confused me,
Unable to realize real from unreal,
You've had enlightened me,
Transformed me,
Now faithfully devoted to you,
My soul and heart being as flexible as possible
Adore you beyond my control

May 30th 1995, Virginia

THE ELEVENTH ANGEL (In Darkness)

A torch rips the inside of my senses and
Feelings,
Fragile soul, cease tormenting me
Comfort this real-abstract mind
With just a loving look

As your eyes, limbs, body and mind stand-still,
They had penetrated me

This relieve is felt by receiving pure essence,
Infinity and wonderful innocence,
That spins around your atmosphere,
Admiring them, they had confused me,

Unable to distinguish real from unreal,
You've had enlightened me,
Transformed me,
As always being faithfully devoted to you,
My soul and heart being as flexible
As possible, adore you beyond my control

May 30th 1995, Virginia

MANKIND IS CALLED

Everywhere there are eyes
Everywhere there are eyes
They are watching
They are listening
No more submission
No more rejection
No more childish jealousy
A battled playground?
A wicked world?
Smell the wisdom
Allow your senses out
Recognize yourself
Yes, see! through the Darkness,
Joyous laughter,
Truly yours

Aug. 26th 1995, Virginia

LET HER VIBES PENETRATE YOU

Come, let her vibes penetrate,
Her sweet essence wrapped by flowing happiness
Throughout her body

Dreams for joyous plays
On the bright crystal-like snow,
Aged couples honoring love and freedom,
Young children resembling angelical creations,
Admire the powerful episodes of life,
Seconds, one by one of the
Everyday struggle for survival

They intensify Past, Present and Future moments,
Oh! Strange sensations radiate those
Colors and dreams from life itself

Come, awakened hearts and
Let her vibes transport thee
To the dimension,
Where all begins to happen

Dec. 14th 1995, Virginia

LET HER VIBES PENETRATE

Come, let her vibes penetrate,
Her sweet essence, a fragile innocence,
Her majestic splendor radiates
Her darkest tears

You had awakened me,
You had penetrated me,
Delighted me

An outburst of joyous plays
Your thoughts paralyzed mine
A stand-still phase

Her genteel smile,
Her sublime intellectual brilliance
Spins around her musical atmosphere

Oh! Fairest creature,
You are A Secret for the Beauty
You are dreams and colors of life itself
No words,
But an exchange of never-ending
Moments that reach me,
Transporting me, to a dimension
Unspeakable your name
Remains in my lips,
For, it holds a special power

Feb. 26th 1996, Virginia

NATURE'S SECRET

Darkness, no more,
The build up of coldness ceases,
Shadows rises,
The ice cracks and melts,
Standstill water slowly flows again,
Wind chills swing, no more
To give birth to nature's creatures melodies

Throughout the blue skies light penetrates,
A celebration of colors takes place,
As mother Nature sleeps,
The earth she is caressing,
And her warm breath whispers,
SPRING

May 20th 1996

THIRST: CAGED TONGUES

Soothing warmness emitted by
The central vital organs,
Fresh/fluid/blood transported across/body,
Skin protects solemnly its treasure,
At the ends of the spine
Round, round, round, slow
The toes float
Belly breaks even

Senses compresses mind
Over human nature
Darkness' powerful light
Unleashed none
Of which perish
In vain ache
Bloody bursts out
My mouth taste
All is none

Aug. 19th 1996, Virginia

55

UNTITLED

In darkest conscience,
I became a part
Of the underworld,
Obscured revelations
Radiant motions from
My limbs
In never-ending sensations
I receive the power

Sep. 1996

UNTITLED

Treeman, a
Shadow of inner
Everlasting darkness
Illuminating, burning
Eyes, love's total opponent
Within this Faceless beard, where light
Coldly burns, auras in emptiness,
Indomitable rivers of blood,
Beelzebub's disease spreads and
Enters, not all but all minds
Tire not no more,
Spasms from
Uncovered fears,
Calling of goodness
Rested I am not

Turmoil of dust of life
Heartbeats-pounds all colors out
Acid corrosion inside
Static nature
Neophobic warriors killed
By their own cease of growth
Suffocate the unwelcome
Interlopers

Oct. 14th 1996, Virginia

AS I RAN THROUGH THE RAIN, THE SAME RAIN THAT SHOWERS MOUNT OLYMPUS

Where Am I?
Where Am I going?
How do I get behind?
If there are no walls
To hang on to!
-Bloody nothingness-
-Shadows of emptiness-
Sleep and Dream
Awake and Live
Manipulate such worlds
Balance the atmospheres
Within your hands

Nov. 18th 1996, Virginia

WHO IS WHO

My body dilates
Within each cell I can feel the recovery
Every rhythm from my heart
Through my eyes
I can smell the atmosphere,
Yet it burns
Her essence soothes the soars of my flesh
Peacefully I invite her soul to
Enter
Welcome the entity she represents
Once long ago I isolated
Only to bloom beautifully again

Jan. 31st 1997, Virginia

NATURA

Nature pushes its way, Neophobic sensation takes over
The ocean embraces the individual willing to take a stand
Once a bitter taste, now floats away
Round blocks of mountains, caressed by green flora
In complete harmony,
A civilization that men/women have the power to alter

Once marked the end of individualism, thus; the
Realization of compatibility between all living creatures

Flowing happiness, the very familiar attraction
Of flora and fauna delights the soul
The physical world in a stand-still phase, slowly
In shadows we glow, a fascination (boiling) deep inside
Fresh orgasms

Jun. 14th 1997, Naples, Italy

BY THE RIVER

Joyous vibration, the flowing river endows
Precious wildlife, rejoicing in happiness,
In total harmony with nature,
Its freedom known, but to a few,
Nature asks for a return of gratitude
To remember, respect, and love all life on earth,
Such as we took and never replaced,
Will we ever be at peace?
Will nature be given its place back?
-Respect-
Will our eyes open once again?
To regain our place under God
Will we remember where we come from?
What we really are,
Children of God in resemblance and similarity
To dwell in Love

Jun. 18th, 1997, Cordoba, Spain

LEAVING SEVILLA

Fields of golden wheat, opening for strong trees of
Lively green rejoicing under the magic sphere

Soft long chains of hills, of dark
Copper ground sway,
As reflecting sunrays
Endow bright green trees
To glow in families

These foundations of earth give birth
To the fantastic valleys

Unknown, yet overwhelming complexes of ideal white
Walls with pastel orange tiled tops hide

High, at the summit of the
Valley there is an ancient watchtower in ruins,
The towers that can be habituated are transformed
Into churches, or one is built in the middle of the
Village

Jun. 21st, 1997, Seville, Spain

ARRIVING

Nature flows in total harmony
At civilization's disposition,
Green pastures of all shades ever imagined
The train roams its way through the earth
Every time is the first time
Shaking the ground, breaking the air
How come the real, is unreal to nature
But becomes real throughout its time in space

Jun. 21st, 1997, Merida, Spain

LEAVING BADAJOZ

Vast flat landscapes of thin and long,
Short-curved and bushy joyous trees,
Starting over round hills of stone
A define air of high plains

Arid lands itch the eye to see further down
The horizon, there, soft green grass in geometrical shapes
Gaps small pieces to give life again, peacefully
Wild flora decorate the hills and flats
Leaving a pure fresh aroma, special to its region
That cannot be forgotten

Pools of soft green pastures laced with golden wheat
Swing, the soft breeze circles,
Pivoting from the inside out, the scene of nature dwells,
Radiates in secrecy

Flowing harmony through the flora and fauna
Holds the eternal, life itself
The strength of survival since creation, the celebration,
With a single blink the rock will drop,
Smoothly in the water, or hit you
In the head

Jun. 24th, 1997, Badajoz, Spain

THE PRAISED MISCONCEPTION

Inside the placenta,
Into broken pieces
Reflections caresses from within shadows
Swirl of mix emotions
Vanished into emptiness
Poked by suffocation
Attributed to chance,
Flow,
Submerge,
Is to simply choose,
Infinity, darkness

Jul. 1997, Germany

UNTITLED

On this earth, the ground extends
Like the heat mirrors in a dry dream
She swings in a warm way
How cougars sense their mothers' breasts
From the thin horizon she shines golden

Jul. 19th 1997, Frankfurt Am Mainz, Germany

THE PENDULUM AND
THE BANSHEE UNDER THE FULL MOON

Thieves plundered thy light
As moonlight tickles skin
Shadows, shapes, swirl, coil
Sensation of swords –splash-
Bright, flesh, soft mass of body
Whips of phallic submission
Scenes of the unreal
Able to stand-still, come, come, come
Oh heavens! Joyous celestial protector
Bound, tie and pull my limbs
Scratch my silk bodacious back
Slowly my blood breaks out
Pleasure bursts
Pain swings
Unleash all windows

Aug. 16th 1997, Virginia

AT THE BAR (In Some Concert @ the 930 Club)

Jungle
Becomes
The new
World order
Of the predators,
Fear, the stand-still gap that comes,
From ousting
That emptiness,
That abashment
Of flowing appetites
A progressive animal development

Nov. / Dec. 1997, D.C.

GIFT OF LOVE

Eyes close upon a splash of blood,
Illuminated, open to welcome pain
Suppressed, lingered – avoided -
Enough to gallop within blindness,
Let not be allowed,
Silent whips, though, when love hurts
Surprisely yea life was spared, being razored stabbed,
Was this sulfur bitter
Taste ever in my mouth?

Mar. 03rd 1998, Virginia

UNTITLED

The shadow of death leaves
Me behind, no less, no more,
Than death alive,
Walking in darkness,
Not even my own shadow
Is with me

The only way to nature
Is from the inside out,
My inner light must
Shine enough to illuminate
My darkness and reconciliate
With the environment

I must fight,
I must love
The sound of the sea shore,
Retrieving after embracing the pebbles,
When the scream that leaves the
Body dry, exhausted and tired, and
The soul too sensible to even
Feel, * hard * stone * cold

Mar. 18th 1998, Virginia

UNTITLED

Time still through space
Clock clicks back and forth
The salty drop burns, as trails down the skin
And leaves,
With pain-life-
Heavy with pieces of the
Broken shell,
A sacred vulnerability
Remains of past shadows
Sways by,
But my soul breathes

May 06th 1998, Virginia

UNTITLED

Past the grey oracle's dwelling cave,
An enigma throbs,
Brings to life the cheering crowd
At a roman coliseum, spectators
Marvel at the god of doom,
Thus rewarded
Marvelous doom

Through the pillars she smiled
The room illuminated with a thousand torches,
As my soul radiated with hope and passion
From only a glimpse
At the eternal beauty
Of this angelical creature

May 08th 1998, Virginia

UNTITLED

Fleshy cloth, heart throbbles
Slow motion facets
Of heavy colors
Silky aromas interlaced

May 19th 1998, Virginia

UNTITLED

Dew falls, a caress
Through the oaks kissing-road,
Sun filters as warmness to the
Heart,
Eyes whispering, nestled your breeze
Interlocks of fire at harmony
Within the torrents of the sea
Protect your past winds, still
They had penetrated me, still
Your deepest fears remain unmasked, still
A bird builds a nest,
The shell will be broken,
When my whistle
Beyond my control, I've never meant to hurt you
Is out of tune, please let me know
Only your angelical creation
Holds the power to love,
I adore you

May 24th 1998, Virginia

GEORGETOWN BRIDGE

Far away lies the light, our dreams
In darkness wrapped
By shadows of the past
At sea, the stand-still phase
Pound! – Pound! – Pound!
Throbbing in this
Dog-day age
We are all
In the storm
We are all
On the bridge

May 25th 1998, Virginia

FIRST BREADTH

How long shall the wrath of loneliness prevail?
When to quench the thirst of the valley's field
Human fertility within the heart and mind
For what purposes is the mind enlightened?
If destruction coils around, awaiting
Constantly stepping behind creation

Is it not an usurpation of free thought, entering completely
To the mind's lonely compartment,
Hollow spaces receptive to human feelings
Hosts
For creativity, yet vulnerable
To even the weakest of feeble minds
Caught in a vulnerable moment
Destruction painfully penetrates
Freeing harm into selves and others

Although time may remain neutral,
Independent with its own flow,
As space expands
Time abdicates by force, space

Now invading
Surpassing the threshold of difference
Blending together
Space and time,
As Rome to Greece

Space conquers and absorbs,
Adopts and spreads
Blinding the past
Nestling a flux
Present becomes a past and into
An eternal cycle,
Its events exhaust time
Suffocating time's individual gifts

Gently
Leaving fragments
Remnants of
Endless possibilities
And scattered memories

Feb. 23rd – 26th 1999, Virginia

UNTITLED

Time slows down,
Closing to the stand-still phase
Remaining motionless
As petals at dawn
Tilt towards the sun, yet
Without moving
Waiting for the sunshine
To bloom
Slowly, the sun warms the petals
Gently opening
Gracefully uncovering,
The guarded heart,
Sun to heart together
Exchanging a mutual love, inevitable
To be interrupted
By thick
Empty
Darkness
Unable to enclose for some time
Vulnerable
To the night's emptiness,
Still, each breath
Vividly brings her radiant image
Throbbing my heart
Freeing my spirit
Confusing my thoughts
With her sight,
Waiting for her

Mar. 8th 1999, Virginia

OH ! FUTURE WHAT COULD THEE HOLD FOR ME (1)

A blend of moist dew and frosty fog
Wraps the environment
Not a soul is seen or heard
Running under the rain through the valley past solitude
Drops flog on the radiant muscular skin
(her-angelic inspiration-muse-victory-faith)
Each heartbeat throbs in rhythm with the limbs
Each foot rapidly pounds on the ground,
Their thump echoes to all sides
As if the ground is shifting

In the mist of grayish clouds on top
Sun rays penetrate throughout the environment
Masking each raindrop with a
Sparkling glow
Casting shadows of emptiness
Alternating between breaths and thumps

Decisively struggling to reach nowhere
Relying on pure passion of overcoming
The obstacles on the way
Doomed by fate
His noble nature immortalizes him
Through present, past and future

Suddenly shadows
Spread and cover throughout the atmosphere
In darkness confusion, overcomes my mind
And my heart guarded by its petals (hers?)
Awaiting the sun
Leaves my soul shivering cold

Unable to discern
Pray from predator
Caught in this storm
Which soaks my fire, and
Darkness usurps inside
Drowning my speech
Flooding my heart with unshed tears
Antagonizing my soul
Tearing its pieces in the breeze
Abandoned by fate

Victory ahead refreshing as youth
Appears in front of my eyes
Could my sight betray me?
Every muscle of emotion
Trembles at the beautiful sight
OH! To have reach paradise,
Gently my body stops running
Only to find a desolate ground
So empty that sounds fall to the ground
Could my sight betray me?

For I must continue,
Resuming my sprint with a feline strength,
There, paradise shines ahead
For the sun flashes between shadows
Though I am almost there (she watches from above)
Could my sight betray me?

Mar. 18th 1999, Virginia

OH ! FUTURE WHAT COULD THEE HOLD FOR ME (2)
(Northern Virginia Community College
1999 Poetry Contest Version)

Pearls of dew sing through the foggy swirls
Flawless winds cross the frosty atmosphere
Racing under the mist through
The valley's solitude shadows
Every heartbeat throbs
Swallows all sound, calling in silence
Interwoven sounds pounding
A patterned thump echoing
OH! The ground is shifting!

Weeping clouds in mourning
Casting shadows of emptiness
Over this pathos of imagination
Narrowing the gates of youth
Relying on pure passion for overcoming
Doomed by fate
Immortalized by nature

The atmosphere gasps for breaths of light
Leaving thy soul shivering cold, and
Petals guarding thy heart
OH! Warm sun, a wait in vain complaint,
Drowning thy passionate lyre voice
Soaking thy creative fire
Flooding thy heart with unshed tears
Antagonizing my soul
Abandoned by fate
Tearing in pieces through the breeze

Yet, Victory lies ahead
Sweet divine youth, strength
Could my sight betray me?
Every muscle of emotion trembles at the beautiful sight
OH! To have reach paradise,
Gently decreasing the pace, only
To find a desolate ground
So empty, where sounds fall down
Could my sight betray me?
Now and Here!
Resume thy pace with a feline strength,
For the sun flashes between shadows
Though I am almost there
Could my sight betray me ?

Mar. 28th 1999, Virginia

UNTITLED

Taste
Its aroma
Swaying fully
Glowing with life
Floating, here it comes, relaxing
Cascades flowing to the natural rhythm,
Hear the waterfall breath, feel the
Familiar warmth,
Under water, swirling
In mesmerized passion
Kissing and embracing
This caged love, was never told

May 24th 1999, Virginia

UNWANTED SECRETS

Like waves that block
The return to the shore,
Superficial sublimation;
Is caressing a feeble submission,
Drowning may be only
Way-out,
Darkest conjugation
Broken off by dry tears
In a fragmented ocean

Jul. 28th 1999, Virginia

UNTITLED

Come near
Let your eyes
Close and feel
The warmness of your essence
Fluxing in a radiant rhythm,
As the sun kisses
Your golden skin
You captivate those around
By your angelical gaze
Which sings of that sweet
Fire within you
An intoxicating nectar
Of life, making
Each breath an oasis
And / where dreams caress
Thy love

Mar. 22nd 2000, Virginia

MUSE 2000 (FAR)

Delighted by your
Angelical atmosphere
My goddess of love
Your inspiration caresses those around
Wherever your path has been
Melting hearts,
Ascending on your wings,
Your essence had
Penetrated me, awakened
Able to see how the earth cradles
Your every step, and
The sun shines your way,
You are the light
That never goes out

May 04th 2000, Virginia

MUSE 2000 (CLOSE)

Your angelical atmosphere sways
Melting hearts, a delight
Of those, whom your love there remains
Your essence -inside –of- me –weaves,
Enabling to feel you
Ascending with your wings, gracefully
Enabling to see you, captivated
By your shimmering eyes, while
The earth cradles your every footprint, OH!
Fortunate sun that shines your way
Endowing an inspiration
That whispers
Your name

May 04th 2000, Virginia

INVOCATING THE MUSE

You're an angelical creature mesmerized
By your inner beauty,
Heaven and Earth rejoice in harmony
They stop, the stand-still phase
To shine on your pearl
Ivory skin, your majestic eyes
Whispers those unspoken words
You say, the warmthness of your
Beautiful atmosphere, radiates
It gives life to those
Around you, insatiable desire,
Musical muse whom makes
Everything possible

2004, Fort Bragg, North Carolina

MEMORIES FROM THE COMBAT ZONE (1) – AFGHANISTAN 2002

All is dark
Sounds of those who suffer
Are heard
In pain I dwell
The joy of laughter
Is no more, but
That of mania escalating
Tired limbs from
Trembles and shakes
To nervousness and anxiety they obey,
Leaving behind memories of yesterday,
Already forgotten
Yet, attached to
The end of one road
The beginning of another
A fatal crash and recovery
Torn between what is and
What is to come,
In Silence I scream,
I need peace

2004

LET THE WIND TAKE YOU WHERE YOU WANT TO BE

Wind blows, caressing
The sand, as waves retreat
Back and forth on the
Shore fluorescent algae
Reflects the moonlight
Sounds of the morning
Have ceased no more
Splash, splash-salt water
Sounds of the ocean soon
Fill the air, its sandalwood
Aroma, sudden bursts of
Stillness takes us simultaneously
To all those places
We call home

2004

MEMORIES FROM THE COMBAT ZONE (2) – AFGHANISTAN 2002

Darkest hours drip by,
Tormenting, this soul
Racing thoughts, caged
Shakes-Spasms-Shakes
Death takes its toll
Crawling slowly, inside
Amazed where clues
Are left around to fit
Like a puzzle,
Emotional - breakdown,
Nerves hissing
Like a rattle-snake
In the desert, burning
Sun, no way out
Hope-Peace-Home the only
Way out

2004

WOMACK ARMY MEDICAL CENTER

Swift changes,
Like the Early Spring
Cold and rough days and nights
Warm in between,
I'm content
Content to be alive
Where every emotion is altered
Plastic - medicine - induced,
Looking in the mirror and
Seeing the person who's taken over my body,
I yearn to find about this person,
Who are you?
It's me, he answers
I have been here for a long time,
He tells me it's been a while
Since I cared about me,
Who is this person? , I asked
It's me I answered,
I smile and observe the world around me
Now it's time, time to live again

March 03rd 2004 Fort Bragg, North Carolina

Oscar R. Rocha was born in Lima, Peru in 1977. At 13 he started writing poetry, at the same time, his mother started working for the Organization of American States (OAS) in Washington, D.C. His family has been living there ever since.

He served with the US Army on the war on terror as part of Operation Enduring Freedom (OEF), with the 3-505 Parachute Infantry Regiment of the 82nd Airborne Division. He is currently pursuing a BS in Molecular Biology in Virginia.